AF226429

Moments On Earth And Between

Narcisa Vucina

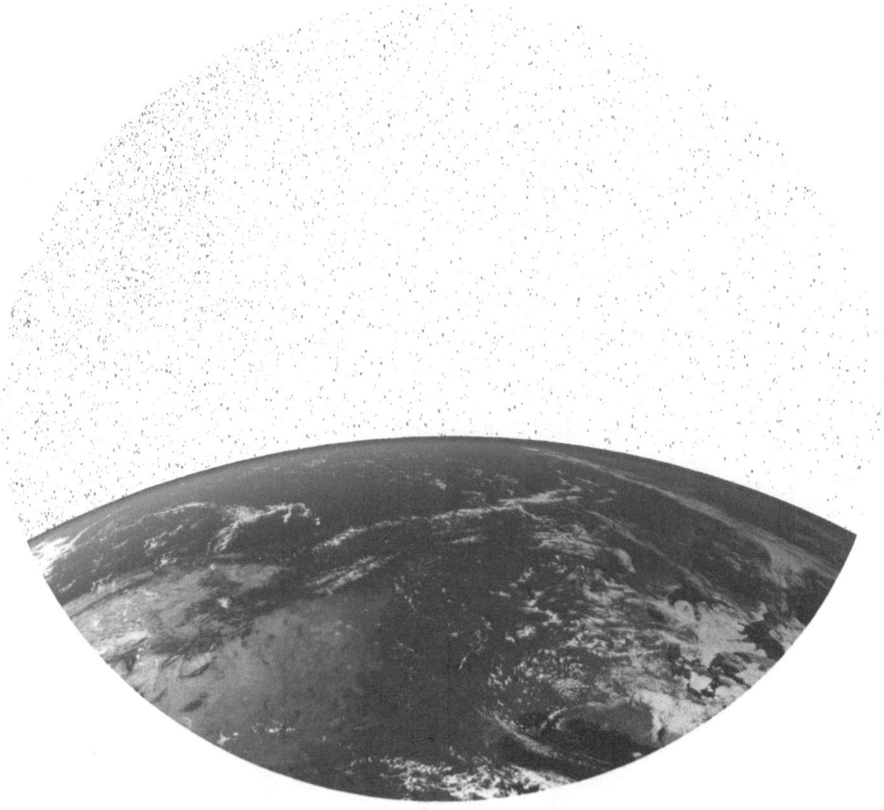

Spuyten Duyvil
New York City

© 2026 Narcisa Vucina
ISBN 978-1-963908-92-3

Library of Congress Control Number: 2026940411

Remember to love

A ROSE

This morning you gave me the sun and the greenery from your lungs.
I deciphered your message of the day.

I hear your laughter that strangles possible rain.

While we're working, killing ourselves with stress, we collide in thoughts,
miss each other, sniff each other.

When returning home, the colors of our lips caress each other with dusk,
knowing that a rose is waiting for us on the kitchen table.

EYES

Eyes
          can't hide
                    anything

Your eyes have already killed my doubt.
Say something.
While our mirrors look at each other's glasses.
While the evening's silence hides its movements.
While we're counting our desires.
          With our eyes closed.

WILLY

I'm crazy about your aftershave.
I'm ready to sell my pride for a touch
of your thoughts on my thighs.

I'll never learn to control my nerves
on a Saturday morning,
when the melody of coffee
kills the sorrows
of yesterday's yearnings.

What a pretty name your mother
has given you, Willy.

THE TICKING OF YOUR WATCH

Sunday morning is praying for our lives,
the church bells tickle the ears, and run away
through the hills, maple trees, and the water
in the lake.

I've heard those bells before in some other
place,
far away from here and I have the same feeling:

I want to stay in this moment
relaxing without meditation,
hoping to hear the earth's
vibrations
every hour and forty-five minutes.

Now I understand why you like the ticking
of your watch when you sleep.

EVENING

You plan to take a bath in 36-degree water.

I urge you not to do it.
I want to smell the sweat on your skin.

There're only three
centimeters from my lips to your
heart,
three centimeters to your soul.

It's healthy to survive,
and take care of each other's lives.

Let it be you and me this evening.

STAY AT HOME

You bring me surprises,
like the northwest
winds.

No, I don't have my phone
in bed at five am in the morning.

Only a pencil,
but I forgot to sharpen it.

Stay at home, don't go to work.
I want to show you the best side of me.

CONGRATULATION

You've been promised to me by some angels,
although I've never seen you.
Vision of you appears increasingly clearly
on the left side of my mind.

Your voice is already singing in my bedroom,
throwing grumpy ghosts out of the pillows,
more powerful than a digital storyteller.

Congratulations. You have won my sympathy.

GOOD HEALTH

We had tea, juice and
soup, we were hungry,
we heard our guts work,

wondered what we were doing to
ourselves,
asking if we were masochists.

You got up,

bought me with your look right away,
ingeniously
took me to bed, massaged me,
convinced me that it gives
the same effect as a 5-mile run.

We can't joke with blood,
it dopes itself
when circulating and extending
concurrently—
you spoke.

I really enjoyed your work.
My feet tickled.
I sweetly relaxed under your hands.

In the end you showed me how to breathe
properly and deeply.

13

It prolongs life
for at least five
years–
you spoke.

LA DIVINA COMMEDIA

I can almost see the sun with my bare eyes.

Where are all those words we once
adored?
Sometimes I'm ashamed that I'm so plain.
I wonder in which house of Heaven
the divine author would place my soul.

Have you ever thought of going to the zoo with
me?
Don't waste your time. Dante is watching you.

JUST FOR TONIGHT

You're lying on a panther skin.
Ready to serve.

The shine of your golden necklace
on your hairy chest gives power
to its foils, ten authentic eagles.

A fair, winged woman flies
over your forehead,
she has achieved your latest dream,
preventing your brain cells
from being renewed.
You must fight for tomorrow.

Unless you write a list
of your tasks for the day
wishing them to be fulfilled.

Unless you have enough fuel
to resist an unexpected coolness
that takes without giving.

Unless your angel hasn't forgotten
to watch over you
in a moment of distraction.

Unless Asclepius has remembered
to heal your weaknesses
with his non-human blood.

Wake up to transform
a potential hatred into euphony,
a simple dialectical play.

I'm coming to hold your defender
from falling onto your panther skin.

Just for tonight.

BEWITCHED BY A NEW VERSION OF YOU

If you forget me
tomorrow, I'll bite you
with
my
mouth
closed

If you wear your yellow
shirt, I'll believe that you've
chosen
another
in your
impulsive commotion.

My colors red,
blue and green
will hit your shining gold
reinforcing my anger and
jealousy.

Look at me with your
irresistible eyes:
your radiance will create
my excitement, amusement
a soft tone in my voice.

Let me be your pillow,
breathing through your vaunted beauty
when windless nights get longer, days shorter,
when dreams steal your imagination.

Oh, rosemary, sage and thyme
my body is on fire, blood boiling,
eyes swallowing your glowing footsteps.
I wish I was a glance
on your necklet
a swallow ready to tumble off it
precarious perch to hang on your shoulders.

I wish I could wash your face
with my moon stone, iron blessings,
baby roses smelling of soreness,
streaming towards thin
shining clouds in deep twilight,
while I'm kissing you under

sleet and thunder, while Pluto admires us
from above
with

its   giant

ocean

THE WEATHER

      It's
raining, raining, raining
mornings, days, evenings,
hours, cats and dogs

dreams,
enchantment
are gone,
love is gone.

Is today the day we restore our pathways,
sculpt our brain to self-regard,
drop the bullying voice,
      that's
      beating,
      torturing us?

Is it at this twilight
  that we'll return to
    ourselves
      and enter
        the state of
        Thanksgiving?

THE SMELL OF YOUR BODY

I just can't remember the last time you kissed me,
squeezing me with your arms and hands,
pushing me towards bedroom walls,
tables, open windows.

If I say I miss those foolish moments, you will
feel flattered without doing anything.
And I'm too proud to ask.

I still believe I found you by the smell of your body.
And no one can take that away from me.

IN MIDTOWN

I will never forget the jacket
you wore when I met you,
near the café on our first
date.
I kept waiting.

You were fifteen minutes late.
You smiled the moment you
arrived.

I didn't know then that you could
still smile when you're bleeding inside.

A TOUCH

The waters of the abundant rivers and
brooks
in the northern hemisphere
burst into an explosion of spherical drums,
tambourines and bells,
showering the resting Redwoods, humming.

The smell of a new beginning melts with
flashing diamonds in the streams.

I jumped down
into the waterfall
without knowing its moods,
its mystical cubicles.

The foaming fluids grabbed my weight,
swinging it back and forth
around the water's gravitation.
A flounce made me meander, fleet.

The waves began to vanish,
caressing me
with celestial firmness, warming my
senses.

When the wetness took all its clothes
off,
the rocks showed their shyness,
but the force of the waterfall still
had its isotopes.

GIPSY PASSION

burning, burning, my blood is burning,
remove my dreams
before they drown me

the first time I saw your face, a
star fell from haven –
my eyes were a witness, I swear

the second time I saw you I faint-
ed from your suffocating
            kisses
the fortune teller's ball was
crushed –
she couldn't see if you'd be
mine
bad sign, I thought

the third time I saw you
I licked your wild skin,
listened to your crazy
heart's beatings, your
flaming muscles –
I could kill you
            with my look,
my lips, swollen breasts,
impatient fingers
the fourth time we were together
you wanted to lend me to your best friend,
even though
  a woman or a car should never be lent to anyone

the fifth time I opened your door
another woman was curling your hair

how dare you play with my feelings!
may God punish you, ungrateful creature!

I heard somebody laughing, my eyes were crying,
the trees took their gloom on

on the sixth day I woke up and my dreams were stolen
I screamed speaking in tongues

forceful knocking scared my heart
I ran to the door with dread deep in my abdomen
the door opened
my Lord, have the owl brought my dreams back?

he stood there
covered with
the morning dew
his eyes bathing in wine
did he regret?
was he ashamed?

His mouth o p e n e d:

> *I haven't slept since we parted,*
> *I wish I didn't love you, but I do.*
> *I'm drunk, miserable, broken —*
> *still, I long for your loose hair,*
> *your melon-like breasts, bare feet,*

swinging around with hips,
jingling with earrings.

I'm dying after your
breath, your
rudeness.

oh rain, oh sun, oh wind, oh soil,
the rainbow in the sky

I threw myself into his arms

IF I WAS A HOUSEWIFE

If I had more honeysuckles from my garden.
If I could change my bad habits, one of them is
following news reports.
If I lived at The Fontenay, once famous residence
in Hollywood.
If I were a housewife, making food without:
nitrites, citrates, benzoates, phosphates,

then "Apples in a Dressing Gown" would be my
favorite.

Don't leave me if you don't like housewives.

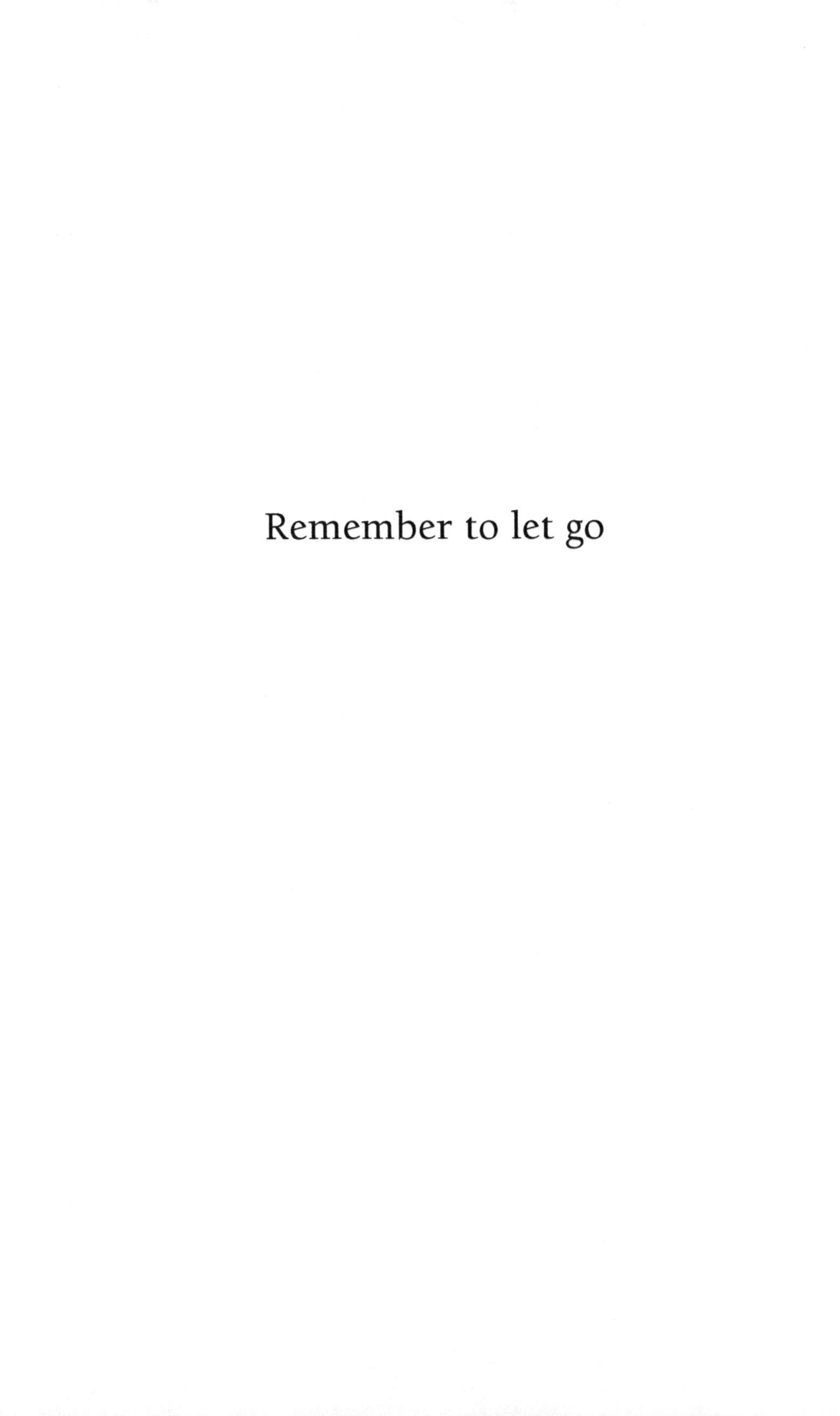

Remember to let go

CHANGES

Quietness has engaged you these days, these
weeks,
you don't talk to me anymore.

Quietness has sold you its best darts and arrows
and you seem to use them with surprising skills.

As if somebody has put a spell on you or me.

YOUR SMILE

The fight has begun, I can feel it
in the air, under the ottoman, everywhere,
even on the little moon Titan.

The raindrops on your lips will need extra energy,
if you want to store them this morning.

Why can't we cry together? Aren't we made of fire?
Take your smile with you when you disappear.

IN THE MOMENTS

Silence is
the worst answer

when you're feeling
hurt

And life
goes on.

But our
footprints remain

in the
moments
of
eternity.

I WILL REMEMBER

I know it's time to go.
I can't put a bandage on
your wound.
It wasn't me
who caused it.
It's deeper than my youth.

I'll remember that one word,
that one look,
the reflection in your eyes.

It still sets my hormones on fire.

You'll remain a mystery to me –
Your muteness tells me I should stay.

WITHOUT SAYING ANYTHING

You've just got up.
I say a sweet "Good morning",
hoping that you'll give me the
last excitement
under the blanket and
say, "Let's try again".

After so many doubts, talks with friends, relatives,
and not to forget the fortune tellers, cats, and marigolds.

You left, without saying
anything
you insisted on doing
all the dying
alone.

THE KNOT

The washing machine was begging
for its **stop** button to be pressed—

shrill beeping,
an impatient cry.

"Hurry, harry—your clothes are ready!
Open the door."

I opened it quickly
and reached inside
only to find the laundry—
twisted
into
a huge
knot:

Dresses, skirts, shirts, pants,
tights and scarves,
bras, underpants, leggings, jeans,
stockings—
all of them clutched in my hands,
a tangled mass.

I stood there confused,
yet strangely mesmerized
by their colors' shimmer:

romance red,

carrot orange,

curry yellow,

balancing green,

calming blue,

purple full of inspiration,

pink with its soft compassion,

restless black,

white with its bright and shadowed edges,

healthy gold,

grey glowing with a metallic sigh.

The huge knot was my **life**.

And I was trying,

piece by piece,

to understand it.

HALF A YEAR

it only takes
half of
our year to
come to
Mars.

half a year
to
realize that we've
made a mistake
that we've
forgotten
to open our
hearts,

give
without
judging,
hesitating.

sometimes
it's too
late to
regret,
to cry,
trying to defend
ourselves
by constructing a
reply.

it takes half a year
to
forgive
to forget,

and continue
living.

Remember to hold on to your dreams

SLEEPING, DREAMING, DYING

Everything is a journey.

Every night we sink into a deep sleep.
Wake up from dreams.
Move to a state of alertness.

Then there are thresholds –
a space between.
One thing ends and another is about to begin.
But we're not quite there yet.

During the day we move through spaces
between,
we mostly don't notice: each moment of
perception,
each moment of thinking.
Even between each life,
if you believe in those kinds of things.

It's a process of transition,
two different states of consciousness:
the night's mind is preparing for death.

Hypnos and Thanatos
are twins.

THE UNITY

After
accepting
the sounds
around
I concentrated on my breath:
breath in, breath out

Random thoughts:
what to do?

Suddenly
lightning strikes
glimpse of timeless beauty

Life is more
than chemistry.
Magnetism, gravity, electricity
are the same kind of stuff
and most of the things in cosmos
are formed of gaseous plasma—
the fourth state of matter.
that can produce
free of charge electricity.
Antigravity,
Galaxies,
Stars, Comets
are not apocalyptic
to the Earth in the
electric space

I HAVE A LOT TO LEARN

I bought a magazine.
I was drawn by the titles:

"Find your Source of Energy".
"Make your Soul in Shape".

There were also a smiling face
of a pretty girl and highlighted
letters in red and blue.

I haven't read the magazine yet,
and the girl is still smiling.

But not like women on the walls
from the Golden Age of the
Pharaohs,
although she acts like she has
seen the fruitful Nile in spring.

She certainly radiates
pyramid self-confidence.

IN FLORENCE

I saw him one summer day. He was standing in front of the city hall
in Florence.
I immediately fell in love with him.

He froze when he saw me. I was flattered that he noticed me.

Suddenly, I saw him naked. Took a few steps forward to admire his
perfect body.

As I got closer, I was unexpectedly sprayed with water.
I was thinking, I don't want to play games with you, crazy man!

When I got really close to him, I felt his firm body.
Then I looked at his face.
He was smiling. I stared, stared, stared.

You crazy woman, how could you be cheated by a statue!

Remember to laugh

IN LOVE AGAIN

I saw you coming out of your Jaguar,
near a trendy restaurant in London's
Mayfair.
In the moment, I thought it was
Jude Law staring at me and smiling,
entering his door.

I wanted to catch your
breath, your momentary thoughts,
put them in my pocket and
save them for sunless days.

I've read about you
in hipster magazines:
your confused childhood,
attempt to study at Oxford,
not your cup of tea.
So, you set aside heavy books
and turn in another direction,
making tens of millions
through hedge funds
and super-prime properties.

And now you're a fundraiser too,
holidaying at Wolf's Fong Peak in
Antarctica, a round-the-world jaunt
by private jet, kite-skiing across
vast fields of snow and ice.

I adore your aesthetic
and mathematical perfection,
your clean-eating habits.

OUR FIRST JOURNEY TOGETHER

Long queues, lost hours, jams, unspoken hatred, anger, irritation.

The National Express' *Driver of the Month* did his best
to make our journey pleasant,
but the lazy flowing dinosaur of trucks, buses, vans and cars
of all colors and shapes was stronger and far more persistent
    moving
            like a
                    snake

stopping when
somebody
got into a crash or an accident.

Sitting in front of the
bus on the M25 motorway.

"We have the heaviest traffic in
Europe"
said the driver looking at us
with his polluted face.

Remember to thank the Universe

SCALAR ENERGY

A fossilized egg, a trace of an ancient gait,
sealed beneath strata of sand and clay,
predating Jerusalem's hills,
predating language,
before human mouths learned
to shape sound from mist.

It is not too late to pray.

Scalar waves can travel
from one hemisphere to another
without loss of power,

faster than
the speed of light.

RADIO SIGNALS

Prepared to enjoy yellow
afternoon,
thinking of sea turtles who are following magnet-
ic routes.

Cypresses, lemon trees, oleanders, sage,
lavenders,
inhale their perfumes, bending to-
wards one another,
ruling the pupils of their eyes.

Having picked up radio signals from
space,
the mind gets in touch with the Sun to get a new identity.

Whispers of birds, insects, humans fly
towards
    the major chords of the Globe.

MUCH MORE

Past – Present – Future
flow into each other, back and forth
like the planet Mars,
up and down, round, and round
outside time and place
like frequencies.

    Black holes bend space-time.
    They create images of the future and the past all at once.
    Their time passes much slower than time on Earth.
    They swallow everything that comes near them.
    They are powerful sources of light and energy,
    using electrical charge and voltage in their atmosphere.
    All the galaxies rotate around them.

    If we could sit on the opposite side of their outer edge
    we could see our picture on the other side like in a mirror.

    The brightest stars live shorter lives.
    When they die, they leave their ghost: a
    black hole.

    The Earth creates electromagnetic waves,
    showing the way to the ascension,
    changing the magnetic field,
    replacing the poles
    from the polar areas to the
        equator
        rotating,
        causing movements of the
        ground,

connecting
the living and the dead.

Life continues
Our planet still has ether –
the substance of the universe,
it permeates all matters.

> We still have happiness.
> We still have feelings.

Remember people you love

DORIS DAY

Day by Day
I'm listening to Doris Day
thinking of taking
a *Sentimental Journey*, on my own, no
matter where, no matter when.

        Just to change the environment,
        use my imagination.

My Dreams are getting better all
the time.

You're probably listening to
Bach or Thelonious Monk,
maybe thinking of the place where
we first met.

It doesn't matter if it's raining methane on Titan, the
largest moon of Saturn
or if Mars has lost vast amounts of its atmosphere
due to the stellar winds released from Corona,
the upper air of the Sun, or whether
Jupiter's moon Europa has an ocean under its surface.

    It doesn't matter if we live seventy percent of our time
    in state of stress, or we are stuck in emotions.

Another ride, another season
will bring me heavenly
sounds, a magic story for the years ahead,
when I will be
in love with the Future.

I must clean my head, my brain,
the hippocampus,
to improve my memories,
do my exercises regularly
to be physically fit.

Gonne set my heart at ease.
> First I'll take a glass of water,
> fantasizing of your *sweet candy lips*.
> Then I'll let my brain consumes more than
> twenty watts, enough to illuminate a bulb.

You'll probably try to attract me with your
irresistible movements.
That's why I'm crazy about you.
That's why I'll find a formula
to regulate my brain and become
part of your fame.
I'll
think, feel, act differently.

Like a child in wild anticipation.

> *Got my bag, got my reservation.*
> *Never thought my heart would be so*
> *yearning,*
> hearing Harry Belafonte somewhere
> far away,
> travelling to his father's *Island in The Sun,*
> my secret love.

JOHNNY

He was born on a cattle ranch
in Texas,
where horses don't talk much,
but whisper.
Where the sun kisses the
people,
their land, grass, rivers,
steady rocks – polite, gentlemanly.

His parents hoped he would become
a farmer –
the family tradition for more than 150
years
 – embracing wildlife, grinding spirit,
knowing the cows by name, praying
for rain.

At 21 he fell in love
with Alice from a nearby farm,
wanted to marry her.
But his parents didn't like the Kings –
they called them
'ill-manned and rowdy'.

Johnny and his chosen one
didn't care what their parents
said,
they tried to defend themselves.

Then –
destiny interfered.
Bad forces crushed
their young hearts.

They never saw each other again.

Johnny left the ranch without
saying good-bye.
Drove away for Silicon Valley,
San Francisco Bay

to study space, quantum physics,
algorithms, robotics
artificial intelligence,
leaving his past behind.

CAROLINE

When she was twelve her parents told her
to be a physician.

Now she's 25 and a top leader.

She's giving out freebies, teaching courses
on giveaways:
how to host your own and how to be invited
to be in one.

Besides, her *3-Part Formula*
keeps her focused during
the recession.
It's doubling her business
in marketing & sales.

Then she asks:

"You can sign up
for this entrepreneur
giveaway right now,
before it's gone.
Giveaways can help you add
1000s to your email list
and you can make money
while you do it".

BILL

Two ash trees in Bill's garden
have been growing together for
years.
He planted them
when he married Ann.

She died when she was 54,
a year after her older
sister,
who loved a man,
that didn't love her back.

Once Bill sat down under the ash
trees
on the newly mown grass.

The trees were whispering
something.
He wanted to know what.
When he found
out, he fell asleep.
And never woke up again.

The ash trees are still living.
But they don't whisper any more.

JANE O'GRADY AND HER DAUGHTER EVELYN

Every time I pass the church, I hear the
bells ringing
and remember Jane O´Grady and her
daughter Evelyn.
They lived on the top of a hill in peace and
harmony.
Got on well together, did not know
loneliness.

People deep down in the valley said
mother and daughter were laughing and
singing and didn't care really
what others were saying.

It was springtime, the trees were green and heavy.
Flowers of the meadow scattered all over so lovely.
You could hear the river dancing, the birds'
chattering, chanting.

There came a handsome fellow asking
Jane O´Grady and her daughter Evelyn
If they could put him up for a night,
no matter if it was in a barn.

When they saw the kind young man all tall
and alluring their answer was:
Yes, of course, there's enough room for you.

He stayed in their lodge not just for one
night, but many other nights, being far
from blue.

The time went on and he remained there
telling them old stories, getting food from
everywhere.

Months went by and one day the bell rang
and one thing happened for sure:
Jane O'Grady and her daughter Evelyn
were in love with the same man.

They began quarreling and shouting throughout
the livelong day, not hearing what he had to say.

When he saw the hatred sparkling from their eyes,
he was ready to run away before sunrise.

It was a bright and sunny morning.
the church bells were ringing.
Jane O'Grady and her daughter Evelyn
awakened and looked for their lover,
calling out for him desperately.

But he wasn't there.
Only a piece of paper
on the table
with the words:

> *I am gone.*
> *Be as you were before,*
> *when you were on your own.*

LINDA

she gathered her feminine posture:

a freezer box with 27 fertilized eggs,
possible human beings,
her descendants' genes.

she felt
free,
content
becoming a fertile
woman,
that was the most important.

now she could
scream,
smile
    gather
thoughts
    as she
was filled
    with
men's
    sperm.

now she could
multiply
herself
without being
dependent on a man.
she could give birth

to babies
without

wanting,
    without
missing
a man's love
or passion.

AVA

Ava was the bright thing
in our quiet neighborhood—
the one light everyone drifted toward.

Whatever she touched
seemed to arrange itself
into some small ceremony.

People gathered
just to feel the weather of her moods,
to listen to her breathing
as if it carried a secret rhythm.

They stayed at her parties
until dawn loosened the sky,
and carried her to bed
as though she were a lantern
about to go out.

Then one day she vanished.

Her absence was a door
no one remembered seeing before.

Some whispered she'd crossed an ocean
in search of a woman
who held her name.
Others claimed she'd stepped
out of her father's store
and into another version of the world.

Six months later
she reappeared at the edge of town—

eyes shadowed,
clothes slipping from her
like memories that no longer fit.

The bright air around her
had thinned to something
no one could hold.

She said she had been to the Mayo Clinic,
where doctors searched her body
as if for a missing star
but found nothing.

Still, fatigue clung to her
like a second skin.

Slowly she learned to rise again,
helped by the stipend
that kept her anchored
to this place.

She turned to the soil then,
growing food with her hands,
joining the quiet movement
of things that live
one inch above darkness.

But Ava never returned
to her old circle of friends.

She moved through the fields
as if listening
for something only she could hear—
a faint summons from the world
she disappeared into.

SABRINA

I hardly recognized her at the farewell reception:
grey hair, visible wrinkles on her face, her neck, sad
expression, red color in her eyes.

She was fired.
After twenty-seven years in the same company.

But it's nothing compared to what I had experienced
in recent months, she spoke.

Her brother died eight weeks ago.

My little brother, whom I loved so much.
I still can't believe he's gone
I might get another job, but I'll never get
my brother back.

Few months later somebody told me that her
mother died too.

She was found froze to death in a park one
cold night.

Sitting on a bench. With her house coat on.
Couldn't remember how to get back home.

SILVIA

You wake up, you've slept too little.
Your phone is waiting for you while you take a shower.

As soon as you've got dressed, you grab it,
you check social media and text messages
rush to the stove, prepare breakfast, quickly.

The phone is ringing.
It knows your fingerprint, your breath, your eyes.

Unexpectedly it deletes the call:
"I have something important to say:

The world is going through a vast change.
Earth's force is speeding up.
You may already be feeling it.
You have a chance to be a part of this
once-in-a-millennium-shift of the planet."

You shout:
"Stop with your preaching! I'm in a hurry,
you silly creature!"

"Easy now. Avoid being angry, irritated.
I have two things to say:

#1 You've found yourself in power struggles.
With your loved ones: friends, coworkers, family.
I'll help you to solve the problem.

Now get in a state of deep compassion.
See their weakness, sadness, defensiveness.
Visit your heart. With concern for them all.
You will see them in another light.

#2 Sleep support: There's a lot going on,
a lot to take care of, piles of work to do,
many decisions to make.
All of it can keep you up at night "

Silvia tried to turn off the phone.
It didn't work.

"This is important! Listen!
Be within yourself for a moment.
Then ask yourself:
What can I do to let go of the power
struggle that drains my energy.
You'll get the answer.

Accept it.

Have a beautiful day.
And don't lose me in some crazy coffee shop!"

Remember to make your heart happy

OUR HEART

I have tried
their help:

a talisman made just for me,
the magic key to help me
step into the shoes of a winner,
words that delete childhood
traumas,
feelings of not being worth it,
bad beliefs about money.

They wrote six pages at a
time,
persuading me that I should
follow
their advice, requesting
more money.

          All these
bombardments
              gave
    me
              headache

              confusion
                depression

              Finally, I found out:
              Our heart has

electromagnetic energy
field which is
5000 times greater than
the brain

Now I put
my hand on my sweat
heart
and
listen to
what it
whispers
to me,
living
in the
Moment
feeling and seeing

with my heart's being

THE SEA AND THE SUN

The sea and the sun hold each other's hands
in the morning being young
full of expectations
ready
to
challenge
the
Milky Way.
During the day
they quarrel
SHOUT   DESTROY   each   other
changing   their **destiny**
moving   borders
killing for a piece of air, affection.
In the evening
they save lives
clean bad consciousness, pollution
bring things in order
regret bad behavior,
call for help
from the giant **Jupiter**.

They sleep in the same bed
under   the   same   star
the same dream
while the core of the **Earth**
rotates

    playing viola
      with its eyes
       celebrating
        the discovery on a reddish rock on
Mars:
dubbed leopard spots and poppy seeds: signs of past life,
but also crying over human bacteria pollution of the planet.

Remember to watch
old movies from time to time

MARILYN IS LAUGHING

I'm dreaming of a sunny Christmas,
far away from my everyday life.

From the top of Mulholland Drive
a filmmaker is buying drugs
in the shadows of cars and trucks,
driving to
nowhere.

Behind Paramount
Marilyn is laughing, sending greetings
to politicians and poets.

Don't worry about movie composers,
their music will break the walls
of secret agents' talks.

SUNSET BOULEVARD

The spell of the sunshine opened our
hearts,
our brains.

      I signed my name
      on your primal instinct.

In springtime
on Sunset Boulevard.

THE CITY OF ANGELS

The mud under my feet has been eaten
by ants and worms.

It was raining fifteen minutes ago,
now the bushes are burning,
like cursed.

It's a long way to The City of Angels, I
must use my fantasy,
or find a bench under a tree.

A plane has thrown rage on
cicadas and chicories
but they spat it out without difficulties.

We are what we sing,
California dreaming.

MOVIES

I've been thinking about you.

I know you are somewhere in the cinema.

But don't knock on my door,
when the night has taken all the good
moments
or if you want to talk about conspiracy
theories.

You can take a pizza with you, if you
come.

Remember to enjoy peace

BACK HOME

Forgotten
our tv is basking in its own flash
 at six in the morning,
your jeans are having fun on the floor.

You're sleeping, having
nightmares.

I'm thinking about waking you up,
you're more amicable at this time of the day
 – scientists have examined our behavior.

I caress your head, hair,
kiss your eyes, cheeks,
moisten your lips.
It's nice to be awakened by high voltage touches.

I'll save this moment.
for future generations.

WHAT WE REALLY WANT

Stay in our piece of
mind.
Don't fly from our togetherness.

From your restless search I suffer
enormously.

Stay in our beam of
light, you'll bless all the
possibilities
and recognize
the number of our destiny.

Stay in our piece of love.

Remember to embrace the future

THE SHOP

When he saw his face in
a shop window
Wednesday, he hurried off,
leaving a feeling of
anxiety and melancholy.

On Thursday he went to the
same shop window
to see if his breath and his
emotions were still there.
Suddenly he saw a shadow of a
person,
then he ran away.

Friday led him to the same shop.
He wanted to return his breath,
the feeling of anxiety
and melancholy back to his body.
Then he changed his mind
and went home.

On Saturday he decided to walk
into the shop to
return his breath and his feelings back to
his body.
When he opened the shop,
he shouted:
'Hello, is anybody here?'

No one answered.
He looked round.
Suddenly – earsplitting
voice from a loudspeaker
            announced:
'Sorry, we cannot help you now.
Please come on Monday at 3 pm
and we will be
at your service.'

On Monday at 3 pm he
went into the shop
and a child about 9 years old came
out of a pink box
and asked:
'What can I do for you, dear?'

Surprised and confused he said:
'Well, I think you took my breath, my feeling of anxiety
and melancholy.
I want my breath and my feelings back.

The child went to a robot in the
middle of the shop,
put something in his mouth and
pressed on.
Now a new voice proclaimed:

'We took your breath from the window
and caught your two feelings before you
ran away.
We came to the following conclusions:

Your breath shows signs of pneumonia.
We've tuned your feelings of anxiety and
melancholy
to the past.
It means you're now only living in the present.
It's called happiness.

As for the shadow, it was me stepping into the future
to follow your soul.
Your fifth-dimensional Light Body is
now a quantum leap beyond
your physical body.
Therefore, you will now need to syn-
chronize your consciousness
with higher dimensions.
Your Light Body now resonates one oc-
tave higher than your third
or fourth dimensional body.

Since you can't be fooled, I want to em-
ploy you:
You can travel to Cydonia on Mars and
explore the huge pyramids
and other structures like the one called
"The Face"
which are the remains of an ancient
Martian civilization.

Or you can control the planet's satellite
which is in orbit
and has been collecting information
from its surface for some time.

And because we have a special offer today,
you don't have to pay for examination of your breath,
only for your soul's renewal.
It is an advantage both for my company and you.

WARPING OF SPACE

Chorus

Once we saw a man walking on an old macadam road,
Wearing a fashionable hat on his head,
A red shirt with golden buttons
Brown trousers with purple stripes.

And he was not on his own.
On his right side there walked a woman
With long, blond hair, wearing a red dress,
Beige shoes and white transparent wings
On her shoulders.

He	She
Finally	
we are together	I enjoy every
I'm so happy	minute, second,
content, grateful	each moment with you.
I was afraid that	You were in a
something dark	miserable state
happened to you.	crying, calling my
I was scared. Now	name. But after the
when you're with me	accident I changed the
I must tell you that	frequency and connected to
I love you,	the invisible, trustworthy
adore	field. You could neither
your rhythm,	see nor feel me, even though
your being.	I touched your rays intensively.

How is it possible?

You can do it too, if you
become greater than your
circumstances, when you
don't think with your
emotions and leave the
third dimension, get in the
heart state, let go,
trust the Universe.

I hope you can teach
me how to
get there!

You have to be consistent and
practice, practice, practice.
Suddenly you will
surrender to space
of thoughts, where all
the possibilities exist.

I have a sensation
that I can learn it.

I'll take you to a
secret place.
It's an old country
house with an almost
broken roof and rooms
that needs to be repaired,
but the old woman
who lives there
is warmhearted,
she'll refresh our tired
bodies
with her food and drinks,
tell some old stories

I've seen the house
once, people were

resting in the garden,
eating, drinking,
their faces shining
in the sun, their smiles
touching a light breeze.

        There, we could rest
        a little, then continue
        our journey
        on the other side
        of the horizon

        Chorus

Once we saw a woman walking on an old macadam road
Wearing a fashionable hat on her head,
A red dress with golden buttons,
Brown stockings with purple stripes.
And she was not on her own.
On her right side there walked a man
Wearing a red shirt with golden buttons
Beige shoes and white transparent wings
On his shoulders.

She had just completed her angelic task,
And he was playing clavicembalo with his
Disembodied mind,
While the spheres bearing infinity
Were moving
Towards the circles of the
L I G H T

Remember to feel free

ON A CHIMNEY

first time
I saw him was from
my kitchen window
one winter
noon

he stood majestically on the highest
chimney
washing himself in the middle of the world
like the most important and precious
inhabitant
of the street,
the whole city, all the air, drinking the water
from the melting snow,
showing his clothes in Gainsboro Gray and
Alabaster White

I don't know how long he was enjoying
himself up there
from the chimney scenery,
but he stood at the same spot three hours
later
and the next noon too,
pretending he didn't
see me.
He was washing his body as if he owned
the chimney, the whole roof,
the entire building,
all the world

A few days
later he was still there
calling for something or someone, admiring
the blue sky, the red roofs,
avoiding melancholy birds, only the joyful ones
with a philosophical look in their eyes

Ten days after the snow was taken by the sun,
he didn't care. He enjoyed changes,
new beginnings, new flights
new heights on some other buildings
some other chimneys

Narcisa Vucina has published poetry collections, short stories and novels. Her poems are represented in Danish anthologies. She has translated books from Danish, English, Croatian/Bosnian/Serbian and vice versa. A self-translated excerpt from her Danish novel *Tildas hemmelige bog (Tilda's Secret Book)* was published in September 2020 in the Los Angeles Review. The novel is translated into American English as *The Button and The Book* (Spuyten Duyvil). The book is also translated into Croatian and will be released in March 2026 in Zagreb at Jesenski i Turk.

Vucina holds a Masters in English from the University of Sarajevo and a BA in Bosnian/Croatian/Serbian from the University of Copenhagen, where she also worked as a lecturer. She studied English Language and Literature at Cambridge College in London, and American English at Hollywood Work Source.

Vucina also worked as a journalist for the Danish Broadcasting Corporation for more than thirty years and interviewed David Bowie, Joseph Brodsky, David Lynch and many others.

www.ingramcontent.com/pod-product-compliance
Lightning Source LLC
Chambersburg PA
CBHW021335060726
47591CB00006B/2031